# Foreword

Nothing helps to accessorize a room quite as much as wonderfully decorated frames. The pairing of frame and picture is a fun challenge and one that can bring out your hidden artistic talents.

Decorating your own frames not only will help to create exactly what you want, you'll also save money in the process. For just pennies you can transform a flea market frame into a piece of art by embellishing with objects found around your home.

Included in this book are ideas for transforming simple frames by adding dried flowers, pressed leaves, shells, buttons, charms and ribbon. A variety of techniques have been used such as decoupage, stenciling, painting, faux finishing, silk ribbon embroidery and lots of embellishing.

Most of these frames can be made in minutes. With your collection of memorabilia and a little help from the following pages, one-of-a-kind frames are as available as your imagination. Use supplies on hand, or look in your sewing box, visit garage sales, antique stores, or craft shops. Match your decor or add dramatic contrast. Frames also make great gifts for new homes, new babies, weddings, Christmas presents, and other special occasions.

Whatever materials you choose to use for making or decorating a frame, add your own personal touch and most of all have fun.

Happy framing!

# The Designers

## Joni Prittie

Joni is a noted craft and floral designer, a painter and photographer. She is the author of several craft and floral books. Ms. Prittie has recently moved to upstate New York. Her designs appear on the following pages: 21, 39, 41, 43, 45, 51, 53, 55, 57, 59, 61, and 65

## Holly Witt

Holly is a free-lance graphic and craft designer who makes her home in Holden, Mass. She has designed many books for Banar Designs, Leisure Arts as well as other publishers. Her designs appear on pages 5, 7, 11, 25, and 37, 63, 67, and 69.

## Barbara Finwall

Barbara, co-owner of Banar Designs is a graphic artist as well as a craft and needlework designer. She designed the projects on pages 9, 13, 15, 19, 23, 29, 35, 37, 47, 49, and 71

## Nancy Javier

Nancy is president of Banar Designs. She has been involved in the craft and needlework industry for the past 25 years. Her designs appear on pages 17, 27, 31, and 33.

---

## SOURCES

**Acrylic Paints**
Delta Technical Coating
2550 Pellissier Pl.
Whittier, Ca 90601

**Blackboard Frames**
Decorator & Craft Corp.
428 S. Zelta
Wichita, Ks 67207

**Fencing, Rusted Tin, Gardening Items**
Kraft Klub
12325 Mills Ave.
Chino, Ca 91710

**Frames**
Cut Out Frames
Apple Buttons
Crafty Productions
2382 Camino Vida Roble
Unit H
Carlsbad, Ca 92009

**Frames**
Wood 'N Needle Crafts, Inc.
140 Thomas Dale
Williamsburg, Va 23185

**Gift Wrap (decoupage papers)**
Gifted Line
c/o Michel & Co.
800 533-7263

**Ribbon**
C.M. Offray & Sons
360 Rt. 24
Chester, NJ 07930

**Silk Ribbon**
Ribbon Connections
2971 Teagarden St.
San Leandro, Ca 94577

**Stencil Brushes**
Loew Cornell
563 Chestnut Ave.
Teaneck, NJ 07666

**Stencils, Mod Podge, Faux Finish Kits**
Plaid Enterprises
1649 International Ct.
Norcross, Ga 30093

**Tin Stencils**
Country Stencils
1534 Marsetta Dr.
Beavercreek, Oh 45432

**Wooden Shapes**
Plum Fun
3427 SE 72nd Ave.
Portland, Or 97206

---

pages.
Principals:
Barbara Finwall, Nancy Javier and Arleen Bennett

Art Direction: Barbara Finwall

Editorial Direction: Nancy Javier

Writing: Sarah Bates

Photography: Joni Prittie, Bob Nishihira, Lin Cariffe

Computer Graphics: Wade Rollins

Computer Production: Chris Nelsen

Copy Editing: Arleen Bennett

Published by

**LEISURE ARTS** ®

LEISURE ARTS
P.O. Box 55595
Little Rock, AR 72215

Produced by

PAGES
P.O. Box 483
Fallbrook, CA 92088

# Table of Contents

# Birds of a Feather

**You will need:**

Frame with wide, flat molding and a piece of
   wood for the shelf
Paint - blue
Spanish moss
2 artificial bird's eggs
1 feather
Sponge brush
Sandpaper
Wood glue
Tacky glue
Glue gun and glue sticks
Image of birds or photo

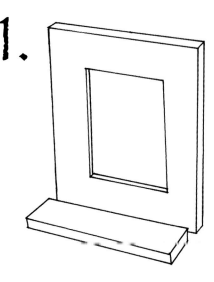

1. Add the shelf( have a piece of wood cut to fit
the size of frame) and glue to front of frame
using a strong wood glue to create shelf.

2. Paint frame blue using a sponge brush. Allow
to dry. Paint a second coat.

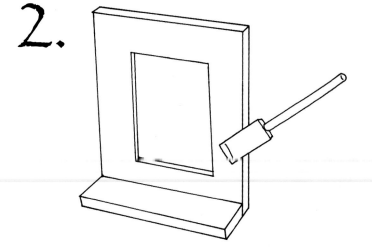

3. Sand frame with a coarse sandpaper to
achieve an aged look

4. Glue feather as pictured.

5. Form a handful of Spanish moss into a nest.
Push in center to form an opening for eggs.
Glue this nest to shelf of frame.

6. Add the two eggs to the nest with glue.

# Birds of a Feather

A charming reminder of spring's feathered gift to life, this simple wooden frame is painted blue to match the background. It holds a print of finches engrossed in their morning bath. For rustic authenticity, their nest poised nearby contains two blue eggs. Spanish moss makes up the nest, though you could use a discarded nest, and a photograph of birds bathing would be just as suitable.

# An English Garden

**You will need:**
Unfinished wooden frame with wide,
   flat molding
Paint - forest green
Two mini half pots
1 mini shovel
Spanish moss
Sandpaper
Sponge brush
Small dried plants or leaves
Seed packet image or photograph
Glue gun, glue sticks

1. Paint frame using a sponge brush. Let dry
and apply a second coat.

2. If an aged appearance is desired - use a
coarse sandpaper to rub away paint
(see photo).

3. Glue Spanish moss to frame (see photo).

4. Glue the mini pots to the frame over the
Spanish moss. (see photo for placement).

5. Insert the dried leaves into pots.

6. Glue the shovel to frame as shown.

7. Insert the seed packet image or a photo into
frame opening.

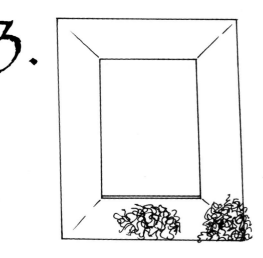

## An English Garden

Surround a vintage seed packet with its own wooden frame and you've captured its beauty forever. Apply green paint with a sponge brush. Vary the seed packets to suit your own color scheme. Find miniature garden tools, pots, dried leaves and Spanish moss at craft shops. Heirloom seeds in old-fashioned packets are available from nurseries and gardening catalogs.

# Who's Got the Button

**You will need:**
Wooden frame with wide, flat molding
Paint - red
Sponge brush
Sandpaper
Buttons - various sizes, mostly ivory
Glue gun and glue sticks
Embroidered fabric piece or photo

1. Paint the frame using a sponge brush. Allow to dry. Apply a second coat.

2. Age if desired, by sanding opening and edges with a coarse sandpaper.

3. Glue buttons randomly to front of frame.

4 Add the appliquéed fabric piece or a photo.

## Who's Got the Button

Antique buttons or just a bountiful collection gleaned from castoff clothing define the theme for this framed bit of folk art stitchery. Glowing mother-of-pearl buttons, and matching ivory-hued companions enhance the red painted wooden frame—a wonderful accent for a sewing room or country sitting room. A photograph could be a more personal substitution for the whimsical embroidered piece and would be just as delightful.

9

# Cotillion

## You will need:

Cardboard frame form (can be purchased at
   craft store or use pattern on page 68)
Gift wrap or decoupage paper with rose images
Marbleized paper - pink
Mod Podge
Pink cord
Pink ribbon
Small ivory buttons, pearls
Round paper doily
Glue gun and glue sticks

1. Cut the cardboard frame form using the
pattern on page 68.

2. Cut out rose images using a small, sharp
scissors.

3. Cover the frame form with the marbleized
paper using Mod Podge.

4. Apply the rose images (follow decoupage
instructions on page 52).

5. Glue cord around inside of frame opening
starting at the lower center.

6. Apply the doilies to each corner as pictured.
Add a cut-out image to each doily.

7. Glue on assortment of small buttons and
pearls to bottom center of frame opening over
the joining of cord.

8. Tie ribbon in bow and glue to frame as
pictured. Add more buttons above bow.

9. Glue cord around outside of frame.

10. Cover back and easel with additional
marbleized paper.

11. Add photo.

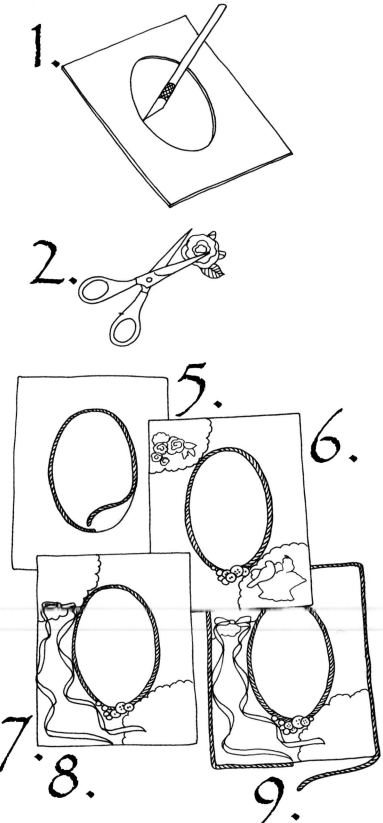

## Tip

If you can't find a suitable wrapping paper or
decoupage paper - you can find lovely images
in magazines, greeting cards and books.

# Cotillion

Sweetly posed for their coming out party or senior prom, this trio of lovely teens form a cameo enhanced by the feminine rose-covered border. Easily made of cardboard, gift wrap or floral decoupage paper, paper doilies, silk cord and pearly buttons, this adorable frame comes together in minutes. Suit the colors and blossoms to the photo.

# Bow Tied

**You will need:**
Small frame with wide, flat molding
Pressed dried ferns
1 yard pink gingham wire-edged ribbon - 2" wide
Mod Podge
Paint - white
Sponge brush
Sandpaper
Rose print or photo

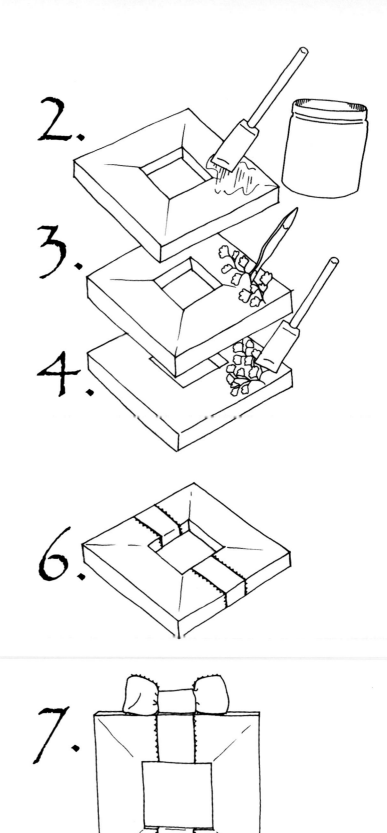

1. Paint frame white. When dry, sand to give an aged appearance.

2. Brush the frame with Mod Podge in the area where you will be applying the ferns.

3. Use tweezers to carefully apply the ferns to the wet Mod Podge.

4. When dry, brush another coat of Mod Podge over entire frame, sealing in the ferns.

5. Apply 2 - 3 more coats of Mod Podge.

6. Cut ribbon into two 4" pieces. Glue to the frame as pictured.

7. Tie a bow with remaining ribbon, trimming ends and glue to top of frame.

8. Insert rose print or photograph.

---

## Tip
Make several of these frames for bridesmaid gifts. Just add a photo of the bride as a remembrance of the wedding.

## Bow Tied

A crisp pink and white gingham taffeta bow adds interest to this framed rose print. Select a frame to fit your print then finish with white paint. Sand to add the aged appearance, then carefully add dried ferns. The entire surface is sealed to protect the ferns. Use this framed floral print as a simple accent in a bedroom or bathroom or any place a glimpse of posies would brighten your day.

# Key to the Past

**You will need:**
Plain black frame with wide, flat
  molding (Wood 'N Needle)
Five antique keys
Glue gun and glue stick


1. If frame is unpainted, paint
black and sand edges to give
an aged appearance.

2. Glue keys to frame as
pictured.

3. Add photo of an interesting
door.

**1.**

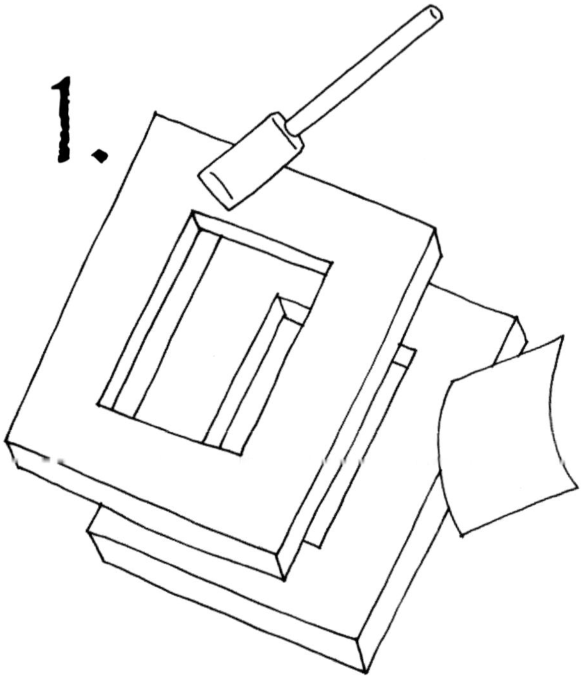

**2.**

---

**Tip**
This frame would make a
perfect housewarming gift.

# Key to the Past

Frame a photo of an interesting or memorable door with this imaginative collection of keys. A black background sets off the old-fashioned metal keys. Sand the edges of the frame to give the appearance of age. Attention-getting, this frame will capture the curiosity of anyone who looks at it and would be a perfect gift for an architect, or friend with an interest in historical homes.

# For Dad

## You will need:

Black frame (or paint a wooden frame black)
6 clear flat marbles
Letters to spell out "Dad"
Mod Podge
Sponge brush
Glue gun and glue sticks
Pencil
Dad's favorite photo of the kids

1. Type letters on computer. Leave plenty of space between each letter for cutting out. If you don't have a computer, cut letters out of magazines. This works just as well. Marbles will magnify the letters, so experiment with different sizes of letters.

2. Place marbles on top of letters and trace around them with sharp pencil.

3. Cut slightly inside this line and place under marble to see if letters need to be trimmed. Trim with sharp scissors or craft knife.

4. Brush a thin application of Mod Podge to top of letter and place under the marble, letter-side up. Smooth with finger. Allow to dry. Letter will be cloudy at first, but will dry clear.

5. When dry, glue marbles to the frame, spelling out your message.

## Tip

Try this technique to personalize a frame by spelling out a name. Use different colors of background paper to add interest to a brightly colored frame.

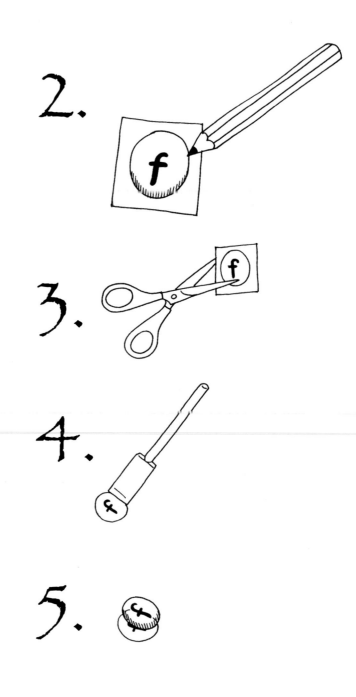

## For Dad

Remind Dad why he spends so much time at that office computer! This clever, personalized framed photo of his two tiny heirs is guaranteed to get him home sooner! Purchase a black frame to make this project easier, or paint an unfinished one. Though this project used black and white, you can change the frame color and paper used for the letters to suit your own color scheme—or Dad's office. Further personalize this frame by substituting the recipient's name.

# Garden Helpers

## Flower Pot Frame

You will need:

Flower pot frame (Crafty Productions)
Paint - blue, white, green, yellow,
  red & lavender
Paint brush

1. Paint pot blue.  When dry, use the end of a small brush to dot with white.

2. Paint leaves green

3. Paint one flower red and the other yellow.

4. Paint the centers of the flowers lavender and red.

5. Add photo.

## Birdhouse Frame

You will need:

Birdhouse frame (Crafty Productions)
Paint - red, white, yellow, lavender
Paint brush

1. Paint the house red.  When dry, use the end of a small brush to dot with white.

2. Paint roof lavender.

3. Paint perch yellow

4. Paint the back, if desired.

5. Add photo.

## Butterfly Frame

You will need:

Butterfly frame (Crafty Productions)
Paint - lavender, white, yellow, green and blue
Paint brush

1.  Paint wings lavender. When dry, use the end of a small brush to dot with white.

2. Paint yellow circles to wings.

3. Paint body of butterfly green.

4. Paint antennae blue.

5. Add photo.

## Wheelbarrow

You will need:

Wheelbarrow frame (Crafty Productions)
Paint - red, white, yellow, green, blue, lavender
Paint brush

1. Paint wheelbarrow red.  When dry, add white dots using the end of a small brush.

2. Paint wheel yellow and center green.

3. Paint leaves green.

4. Paint one flower blue, the other lavender. Paint centers of flowers yellow.

5. Paint the back if desired.

6. Add photo.

## Garden Helpers

Keep the cheerful faces of your garden assistants nearby in colorful frames to remind you of sunny days and helping hands. The birdhouse, butterfly, flower pot, and wheelbarrow are ready-made to hold a photo, but come unfinished. Use the colors chosen for the project or select shades which match your decor. These frames are simple to paint and easy to mount photos. An easel on the back lets you display them anywhere.

# Floral Medallions

## You will need:

Frame with wide, flat molding
Paint - white, green
Sea sponge
Wrapping paper with medallions
   (or floral paper)
Mat
Craft glue
Brush
Mod Podge
Spray mount adhesive

1. Paint frame with white paint. Let dry.

2. Mix green paint with 1/4 water and lightly sponge this wash on the frame by pouncing gently allowing some of the white to show through (see photo).

3. While frame is drying, cut out medallions (or flowers) from wrapping paper. Brush Mod Podge to back of cut out images and apply randomly to sponged frame, one at a time. Smooth out any wrinkles using your fingertips. Let dry.

4. Brush entire frame with a layer of Mod Podge. You may wish to apply 2 - 3 coats.

5. Cut a small mat board 11/2" on all sides for liner . Spray mat board with spray adhesive and apply strips of ribbon to cover mat, mitering corners.

## Floral Medallions

Green sponge painting becomes the background for this lovely view of a garden walk. Floral medallions have been added to create a garden theme. A dark mat, embellished with printed ribbon completes the picture.

# All Fenced In

**You will need:**
Rough wooden frame
Miniature fencing (available in one
  yard lengths)
4 rusted tin stars
Glue gun and glue sticks

1. Measure the length of each side of frame.

2. Cut a length of fencing to fit each side.

3. Glue the longest length of fencing to a long side of the frame.

4. Next, glue a short length, overlapping the last one.

5. Continue in this way, securely gluing several of the fence posts to the frame and to each other.

6. Glue the rusted tin stars to each corner.

7. Add the image or a photograph.

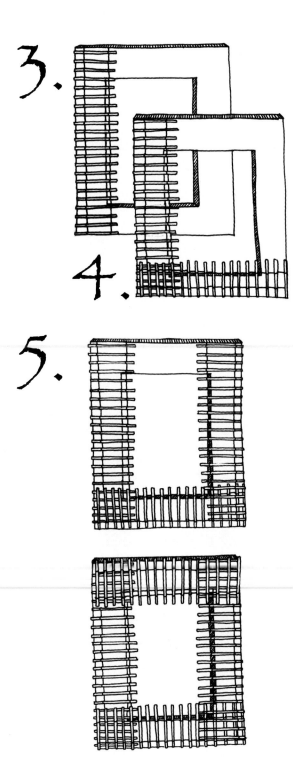

## All Fenced In

Find the fencing material and tin stars for this unique frame at a craft shop. A good way to cover an old or damaged frame you have on hand, this woodsy creative solution enhances old photos, or new ones. Use this technique to bring a bit of country flavor to a man's den or office or to a modern setting.

# Woodland Frame

## You will need:
Cardboard frame form with oval opening
   (pattern page 66)
Bark
Twigs
Acorns or pods
Paint - brown
Glue gun and glue sticks
Sponge brush

1. Cut frame form using the pattern on page 66.

2. Glue flat pieces of bark entirely covering front of frame. Trim bark with a large scissors or craft knife to fit the design and shape of frame.

3. Glue twig pieces around outside edges of frame.

4. Glue on acorns, pods and twigs as shown.

5. Paint back and easel of frame with brown paint.

6. Insert image or photo.

---

## Tip
Many natural items found in your backyard or on a hike can be incorporated into frame designs - dried leaves, twigs, eucalyptus pods, dried berries, mosses, etc. To remove bugs or other unpleasant creatures from natural items - microwave on high for 3 - 4 minutes

# Burlap and Buttons

## You will need:
Frame form with oval opening
   (pattern on page 66)
Burlap
Wooden hearts and buttons
Paint - red, green, yellow
Embroidery floss - black
Thin batting
Tacky glue
Glue gun and glue sticks
Marking pen

1. Cut the frame form using pattern on page 66.

2. Paint the wooden shapes (see photo or use your own color scheme).

3. Trace around frame form onto batting with marking pen. Cut out.

4. Glue batting to front of frame form using Tacky glue.

5. Cover the frame form with the burlap (see instructions for Fabric Covered Frames on page 76).

6. Blanket stitch (stitch instructions on page 79) with the black floss around the oval opening and the outside edge.

7. Glue on the painted wooden shapes (see photo).

8. Add photograph.

## Woodland Frame

Wonderful reminders of a hike in the woods, nature elements make up the border of this country-style frame. Add bits of bark, twigs, pods, berries and mosses to create your own authentic rendition. Start with a simple wood frame, or cut one from heavy cardboard as we did here.

## Burlap and Buttons

Country touches embellish this burlap frame which surrounds a vintage photo. A beginner can manage the embroidered blanket stitch, and the wooden hearts and buttons are added with a glue gun. Instant folk art!

# My School
# Picture

## You will need:

Green frame with wide, flat
    molding , (Wood 'N Needle)
Four small pencils
Four apple buttons (we added
    thread to the button holes)
Glue gun and glue sticks

1. If using a plain wooden
frame, paint it a forest green
(or color of your choice).

2. When dry, sand the edges
of the frame to achieve an
aged look.

3. Glue the apple buttons to
each corner and the pencils as
pictured.

4. Add a school photo.

(Tip: This project is easy enough for a child to do. It would
make an excellent teacher's gift or a gift for grandma).

## My School Picture

What a way to show off the beautiful changing of time depicted by school photos. Dark green paint on a wide wooden frame highlights the shiny yellow pencils sharpened to fit the sides. Red apple buttons add a bright touch at the corners. Paint the frame or buy one already painted in your favorite color. This project is kid-friendly, and would make wonderful gifts for all the doting grandmas!

# Class Photo

**You will need:**
Blackboard frame
Class photo
Mod Podge
Plaid fabric
Large button
White chalk
Glue gun and glue sticks
Sponge brush
Pinking shears

1. Cut background from the class photo so that it fits within the frame (see photo). You may wish to have a color copy made so that you don't ruin your original photograph. Also you can reduce or enlarge the photo to fit your particular frame.

2. Brush Mod Podge on reverse side of the photo and the slate using the sponge brush and apply photo to blackboard. Brush Mod Podge on front of photo and smooth out any wrinkles with fingertips. You could also apply the photo using a glue stick.

3. Cut edges of fabric with pinking shears and tie in a bow. Glue bow to upper edge of frame and glue button to the center.

4. Write message with chalk. This could also say "Class of '99" or "My Second Grade Class".

# Number One Teacher

**You will need:**
Blackboard frame
2 Wooden apple shapes
Paint (Ceramcoat) red, brown, green, white
Paint brush
Glue gun and glue sticks
Chalk

1. Paint the apples red. Brush with white to add highlights. Brush with brown to add shadows.

2. Paint stems brown and leaves green.

3. Add veins to leaves with brown.

4. Glue apples to frame as pictured.

5. Write message to teacher using chalk.

## Other teacher sayings which may be used:
A + Teacher
Teachers Make the Grade
Teachers Rule!
Teaching is a work of the heart
World's Greatest Teacher
Teachers are special
To Teach is to Love

## Teacher's Pet

Two blackboard frames with ruler borders form the basis for these two gifts for a favorite teacher.  Add two bright red apples or a carefully cut class photo along with a sincere compliment and a memorable gift is created.

One frame has been decorated with a jaunty plaid bow and a button, the other with teacher's favorite fruit!  Add your own words to this gift, or choose from one of ours.  Either way, this tribute will be appreciated.

# Puzzled?

### You will need:
Black wooden frame with
 wide, flat molding
Inexpensive small puzzle
Glue gun and glue sticks

1. Paint the frame to match
the puzzle pieces you will be
using.

2. Choose several pieces of
the puzzle and glue to the
front of the frame in a
random design (see photo).

3. Cut out the picture on the
top of the puzzle box and
use this image to frame. Or
you may choose to frame a
photograph instead.

### Tip
Old puzzles are easy to find at garage sales and thrift
shops - and for this project, it doesn't matter if all the
pieces are in the box!

## Puzzled?

Charming decor from a puzzle is easy with this colorful project. A black wooden frame is the base. Bright puzzle pieces glued to the surface add whimsy. Use this unique frame to enclose an interesting puzzle box lid to enhance your decorating scheme or give as a gift to a puzzle addict. This treatment would be terrific surrounding a photograph, too.

# Baby Face

## You will need:
Small frame with wide, flat molding
3 dozen 1/4" white pom-poms
Glue gun and glue sticks

1. This frame was purchased - but it could be reproduced by painting a square frame yellow and adding a wooden bunny painted white and glued to a small spring.

2. Position pom-poms on frame.

3. Glue the white pom-poms to the front of frame as pictured.

4. Insert baby photo.

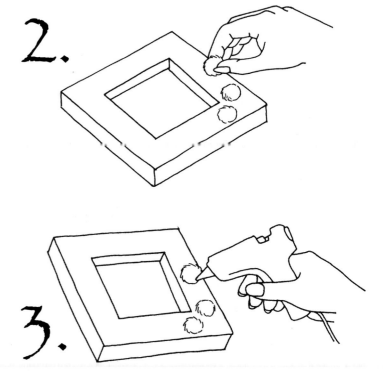

### Tip
This frame would be an ideal baby shower gift along with a fabric covered photo album also covered with pom-poms.

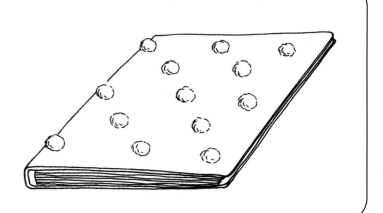

# Baby Face

Looking out from its cheery yellow frame embellished with snowy white pom-poms, baby smiles delightfully. Purchase a painted frame, or paint one to match your nursery color scheme. A little white bunny adds to this clever project, but you could add any nursery animal that suits the design. This sweet frame is simple enough to make in quantity for gifts.

# Silk Ribbon Heirloom

**You will need:**
Cardboard frame form (see pattern page 80)
White moiré fabric
Pink cord
Embroidery floss -
   light green, pale yellow
Silk ribbon -
   3 yards purple - 4mm
   3 yards light pink - 4mm
   2 yards mauve - 7 mm
Sharp embroidery needle No. 24
Thin batting
Craft glue or glue gun

1. Cut cardboard frame form using pattern on page 80.

2. Transfer embroidery pattern to fabric using an iron-on transfer pen (follow manufacture's instructions).

3. Stitch the design following instructions on page80.

4. Cut fabric 1" larger than frame.

5. Cover the frame form following instructions for Fabric Covered Frames on page 76.

6. Glue cord around inside opening of frame and outer edge.

7. Cover the back and easel with the remaining fabric.

## Silk Ribbon Heirloom

Make a family collectible that will be treasured from generation to generation. Your own silk ribbon embroidery worked on creamy moiré creates a beautiful and feminine frame. Add a beautiful braided trim for a finishing touch. Display one of your own vintage photos or a contemporary portrait. Either way, the result will become an instant heirloom.

# Floral Drama

You will need:

Cardboard frame form
 (see pattern on page 68)
Black and floral chintz fabric
Black and white stripe fabric
Wire-edged ribbon - ombre
Mauve braid
Angel charm
Thin batting
Craft glue
Glue gun and glue sticks

1. Cut the cardboard frame form using the pattern on page 68.

2. Glue batting to front of frame form.

3. Cover the frame form with the fabric following the instructions for Fabric Covered Frames on page 76.

4. Glue the cord to inside opening of frame and around outer edge.

5. Cut a strip of striped fabric about twice as long as the circumference of the frame form and double the width of the desired ruffle. Fold it in half widthwise and glue it to the back of the frame form, pleating as you go.

6 Crumple and drape ribbon as shown in photo. Glue in position.

7. Glue angel charm to ribbon at lower center of frame (see photo).

8. Cover back and easel with remaining fabric.

36

## Floral Drama

For a colorful and dramatic accent, this frame uses two chintz fabrics, braid, and a cherubic charm to create its interest. With its gathered ribbon, this frame is the perfect complement to a black and white or sepia photograph. Its oval center draws the eye in towards the cameo print. This frame is easier to make than it looks and is sure to be an attention getter.

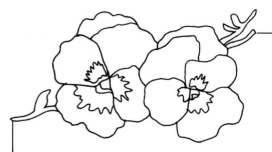

# Floral Garden

**You will need:**
A mirror with wide, flat molding
Assortment of dried spring flowers
    including pansies
1 yard silk ribbon - 1 1/2" wide
Green moss
Glue gun and glue sticks
Silica gel (optional)

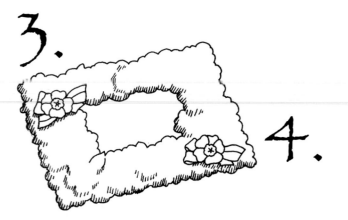

1. Glue on moss completely covering the frame.

2. Glue on flowers one by one until the frame is completely covered.

3. Cut the ribbon in half and tie two bows. Glue bows to two corners of frame.

4. Glue a flower to the center of each bow.

(Use Silica Gel to dry your own blossoms - see page 38.)

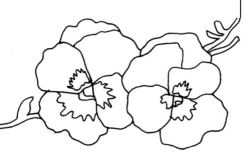

# Floral Garden

"Mirror, mirror on the wall…" Surrounded by dried flowers, no matter who peers into this mirror, their image will smile back. Capture the beauty of dried flowers on a moss-covered background. Start with a plain mirror with a flat wooden frame, carefully add your own bouquet using a glue gun. Dry your own blossoms or purchase from a craft store. Silk replicas would also be perfect. Display this beautiful frame wherever you want a bright reflection.

# Pretty Pansies

**You will need:**

Frame with wide, flat molding

Green moss

Dried pansies

Silica gel (optional)

Glue gun and glue sticks

1. Attach green moss completely covering the front and edges of frame using a hot glue gun.

2. Glue pansies one at a time over the moss.

3. Use caution when handling this frame as it will be very fragile.

## Drying your own flowers

Flowers for drying should be harvested when the blooms are in peak condition, just prior to reaching their prime. They should be picked around midday when they are dry. Some flowers such as peonies, roses and statice will continue to open and will keep opening after being cut.

### Desiccant method:
Cover flowers in silica-gel crystals for 1 - 3 days.

### Microwave method:
Spread flowers on paper towel and heat on low, 1 - 3 minutes.

## Pretty Pansies

Lovely purple pansies surround this frame displaying a print as pretty as the posies. The pansies are dried and then carefully glued to the frame to achieve this lovely creation. Purchase pansies already dried or dry your own.

# Together Forever

**You will need:**
2 identical frames with flat molding
Paint - green, rose
Cloth tape
Green ribbon - 1/2 inch wide
Tacky glue
Paint brush

1. Mix green paint with 1/2 as much water. Do the same with the rose paint.

2. Paint the front of the frames with the green wash.

3. Paint the sides of the frames with the pink wash.

4. Allow to dry.

5. Paint a loose curvy line around frame opening using full strength of rose paint.

6. Hold frames on top of one another with front sections facing and apply a length of cloth tape along one edge to hinge the frames together.

7. Cut two 10" pieces of ribbon and tie small bows with long streamers. Tie knots in the streamers.

8. Glue the loops of each bow to frame fronts, positioning on frame to look like hinges.

**6.**
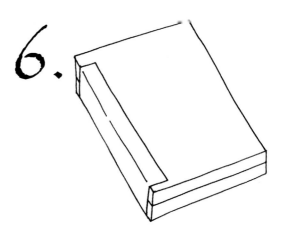

**7.**
**8.**
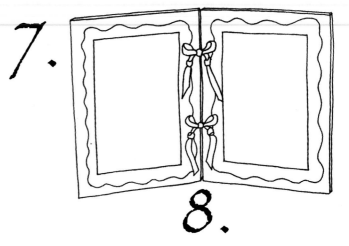

## Together Forever

Two inexpensive wooden frames have been hinged and be-ribboned in this beautiful duo. A wash of green and delicate pink add the colors which compliment the prints chosen for this combination. Green ribbon adds the accent.

# Sunny Yellow Summer

**You will need:**
Glass clip frame
Bright yellow paper
Floral motif wrapping paper
Spray mount adhesive
Tacky Glue
Mod Podge
Sponge brush
Small sharp scissors

1. Disassemble a glass front clip frame. Set glass aside.

2. Measure cardboard and cut yellow paper 1" larger.

3. Apply spray adhesive to front of cardboard backing piece.

4. Apply the paper on sprayed surface. Fold paper over to the back of cardboard and secure with tacky glue.

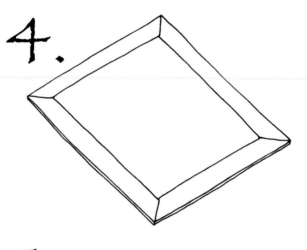

5. Cut out floral shapes.

6. Center your photo or image (we used a greeting card) and glue using a thin layer of tacky glue.

7. Brush Mod Podge with sponge brush on back of flowers and apply to frame randomly surrounding the image. Smooth down with fingertips to avoid wrinkles.

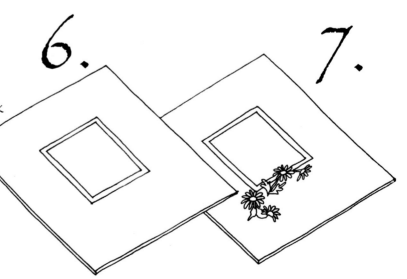

8. Allow to dry. Place glass on top and fasten with frame clips.

## Sunny Yellow Summer

Bright and cheery with floral cut-outs, this frame captures memories of summer fun. Start with a purchased glass front clip frame, add yellow paper and big red and blue posies, and just glue on your photograph. Create the frame to compliment the photo for an exciting result. Use vintage florals for nostalgia, or contemporary floral art for a modern touch.

# For Four Legged Friends

**You will need:**
Small frames with wide, flat molding
Pet stencils (Plaid)
Paint - lavender, green, white
Sponge brush
Stencil brush
Sharp black marker

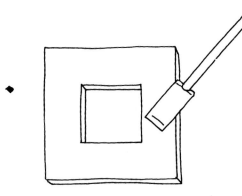

1. Paint frames using sponge brush - 2 coats.

2. When dry, stencil the animal images with white paint.

3. Add the facial details using the black marker.

4. Insert photos of favorite pets.

### General Stenciling Instructions

1. Tape the stencil to the object to be painted. Apply paint to brush and then dab the brush on a paper towel so that the brush is almost dry.

2. Hold brush vertically and use either a dabbing or swirling motion. Start at the edges of the stencil while you have more paint on your brush and let it get lighter (less paint) towards the center. This will give you a shaded effect.

3. When finished painting, peel away the stencil before the paint is completely dry to prevent the paint from cracking.

## For Four Legged Friends

Family members with four legs are endearing additions to your life. Don't forget to frame their most precious moments, too. Small frames with wide flat surfaces are perfect for this project. Pet stencils make this project easy. Find them at craft stores then add your own pet's special smile with a sharp-tipped marker.

Tip
Practice your stenciling technique on paper first. This will acquaint you with the application technique.

# Gardening Frame

**You will need:**
Frame with wide, flat molding (Wood 'N Needle)
Paint - forest green, white
Mini gardening gloves
Gardening stickers
Sea sponge
Mod Podge
Glue gun
Sponge brush

1. Paint frame forest green using the sponge brush - 2 coats.

2. Lightly pounce over the frame using a small section of the sea sponge and white paint.

3. Glue gardening gloves to upper left corner of frame slightly overlapped.

4. Apply gardening stickers to lower right side of frame.

5. Insert a gardening print or a family photo.

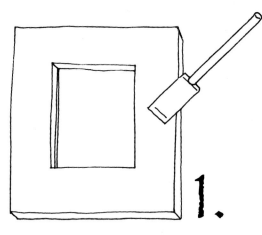

# Gardening Frame

When you can't be in the garden, this delightful keepsake of days spent with the perfect pair of helping hands, serves as a welcome reminder. Sponge painting over a deep green frame sets the stage. Add miniature garden gloves and a selection of garden stickers. Tiny garden tools would be a nice addition, too.

# Dainty Bouquet

## You will need:

Glass or plastic frame with an
  embossed surface
Paint - white, pastel pink, green,
  yellow, orange and light green.
Small paint brush (liner)

1. Mix all colors of paint with a small amount of white.

2. Apply brush strokes of green to frame front. Add flower buds of pastel colors following photograph.

3. Add leaves with a lighter shade of green using small brush strokes.

4. Paint tiny white dots using the end of a small brush.

## Tip

If you're hesitant to paint with a brush, you might try using dimensional paints which are now available with fine tips to do more delicate painting. Look for dimensional paints that are for painting on glass. It's a good idea to store dimensional paints upside down. This will help the paint to flow more easily. Empty egg cartons can be used for storing dimensional paints.

50

# Dainty Bouquet

Delicate and feminine, this project starts with an embossed glass or plastic frame. Pastel posies added with a light touch, combine with soft white dots to create an effect that sets off a complimentary watercolor print. A thoughtful gift for someone who loves flowers, or just a colorful addition to a girl's bedroom or bath, this project becomes a work of art when finished.

# Tissue Decoupage

## You will need:
Tissue paper - gold, silver and copper
Mod Podge
Sponge brush
Spray glitter

1. Tear the tissue paper into small, random pieces.

2. Brush Mod Podge on frame and quickly press pieces of tissue to frame, smoothing out any wrinkles with fingertips. If Mod Podge dries, apply more until frame is completely covered with the tissue pieces.

3. When dry, brush on 2 to 3 coats of Mod Podge allowing to dry between applications.

4. If desired, spray a thin layer of spray glitter to finish.

## Alternative Ideas

Use pastel colored tissue paper to create a frame for a baby's photo. Use red and green tissue for a Christmas frame to hold a treasured holiday family photo. Use floral printed tissue paper for a very feminine style frame.

## Decoupage Instructions

1. Choose images from greeting cards, gift wrap, magazines, old photographs, calligraphy, etc.

2. Cut out the images with a sharp, pointed scissors.

3. Use a sponge brush for applying Mod Podge. Coat the back of the image. Place it on the object to be decorated and paint over it with the Mod Podge. This wet layer will allow your fingers to slide easily over the surface to rub out wrinkles, paper folds and excess Mod Podge.

4. If you want images to wrap around the edge of an item, add extra Mod Podge and mold around the edge with your fingers.

5. Let dry and add more coats of Mod Podge until you achieve the desired effect.

6. Other objects can be glued to the decoupaged items such as charms, buttons, bits of lace, etc.

## Tissue Decoupage

Wonderfully metallic hues of gold, silver, and copper tissue paper are used to create this glamorous frame. Glitter adds an exciting touch. This project uses a decoupage technique which is easy to do and yields successful results, even for a beginner. Follow our project instructions, or select tissue paper that suits your color scheme. Either way, the frame becomes a unique expression of your creativity.

# Apple Time

**You will need:**
Frame with wide, flat molding
Assorted artificial mini apples (or other fruits)
Green moss
Velvet blossoms and leaves
Glue gun and glue sticks

1. Cover frame with green moss using glue gun.

2. Glue the fruits randomly over the moss using glue gun to completely cover the frame.

3. Glue the velvet leaves and blossoms in between the fruits and across the back of the frame.

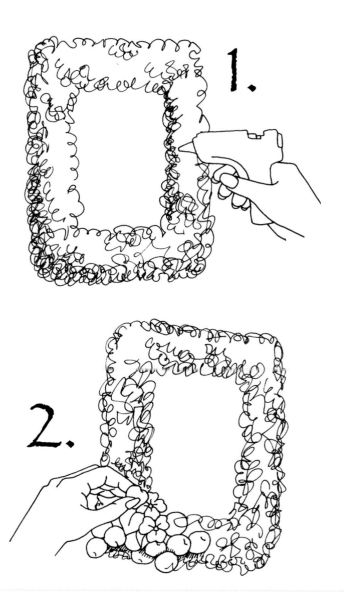

### Tip
Completely cover the frame with the velvet leaves instead of the moss. Then add the apples. Other artificial fruits could be used such as cherries. For a Christmas frame, glue on dried evergreens, small pinecones and tiny ornaments.

## Apple Time

A bountiful harvest of apples, blossoms and leaves create a lush frame for this impressionist print. Hang this beauty on a wall or prop it up wherever you want a bright color spot. We've used apples, but you could substitute any other suitable miniature fruit, such as pears or grapes. Green moss forms the background on the wide frame, creating a secure base for the mounds of luscious fruit.

# Fragrant
# Cinnamon Frame

**You will need:**
Frame with wide molding
6 dried orange slices
1 dz. 6" cinnamon sticks
Dried roses or other
   burgundy flowers
Glue gun and glue sticks

1. Arrange cinnamon sticks on frame and cut them to fit the molding (see photo). Use a knife with a serrated edge.

2. Glue cinnamon stick pieces covering all of molding.

3. Cut orange slices into quarters and glue to each corner of frame and in the center top and bottom. See photo for placement.

4. Arrange and glue the dried flowers over the orange slices.

5. Add a botanical print to coordinate with the finished frame.

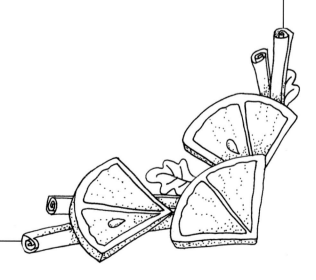

## Fragrant Cinnamon Frame

Provide beauty and fragrance to your kitchen with this spicy cinnamon covered frame. Add dried orange slices and burgundy flowers to complete the picture. A botanical print is the ideal subject to be displayed in this scent-sational frame.

# Seashells by the Seashore

## You will need:

A large framed mirror with a
  wide molding
Assortment of shells
Glue gun and glue sticks

1. Select a nice assortment of
shells that will complement one
another. Collect them yourself
at the seashore or purchase
them at a craft store.

2. Starting in one spot on the
frame, glue the shells
overlapping as you go.
Completely cover the frame
with the shells.

## Tip

There's an array of found
objects besides shells that
would be suitable for covering
frames.  Here's a list of
possible decorations:
  rope or gold cord
  dominoes
  macaroni
  seeds
  flat marbles
  leaves
  potpourri
  twigs and bark
  bottlecaps
  charms
  beads
You may think of other items
to decorate frames. Let your
imagination go and see what
you can come up with.

## Seashells by the Seashore

Recycle a mirror with a wide frame by attaching a wonderful collection of shells for a terrific addition to decor with a nautical theme. As an accent in a bathroom or hallway, the soft pastels of shells bring nature into a room. The mirrored reflection lights up the area. Cover the frame completely for the most stunning effect.

# Royal Velvet

**You will need:**
Frame with wide, flat molding
Red velvet
Spray mount adhesive
Sharp scissors
Gold cord
Gold tassel
Craft glue

1. Cut velvet 1" larger than your frame. Cut corners of fabric on a miter.

2. Spray the adhesive on front and sides of frame.

3. Apply the piece of velvet to the front of the frame.

4. Fold the sides of the fabric to the back of frame and glue.

5. Cut an "X" into the center of frame's opening. Cut to 1/4" of each corner. Fold this fabric into opening and around to back and glue as you go using craft glue.

6. Measure frame opening. Cut cord to this size and glue around opening. Glue gold cord around front of frame about 1" from opening.

7. Glue tassel where cord ends meet.

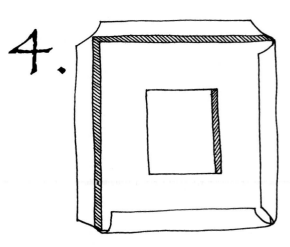

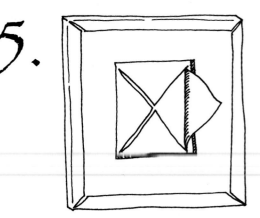

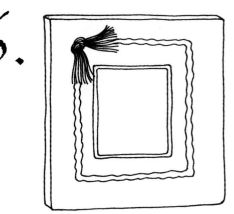

# Royal Velvet

Red velvet and gold, what richer combination exists? For a royal portrait or your own little prince or princesses, this project is perfect.

Gold cord and tassels add an elegant touch. For even greater sophistication, use black velvet.

# ABCs

You will need:
Cardboard frame form with oval opening
Plaid fabric
Alphabet pasta
Wooden shape - school house
Paint - red
Glue gun and glue sticks
Craft glue
Thin batting

1. Cut frame form using pattern on this page.

2. Glue batting to frame form.

3. Cover frame form with the plaid fabric (see instructions for Fabric Covered Frames on page 76).

4. Glue the alphabets to frame (as pictured).

5. Paint schoolhouse red. Allow to dry.

6. Glue schoolhouse to frame and add a school photo.

## Tip
Instead of using the alphabets for adding "ABC" to frame, use the letters to spell out the child's name and the grade. This is a great project for children. Not only will they have their own frame when they're finished, but they can use the alphabet pasta to spell out words and learn as they're crafting. When finished, add the left-over pasta to a home-made soup.)

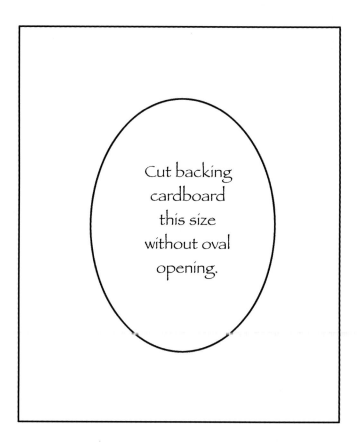

Cut backing cardboard this size without oval opening.

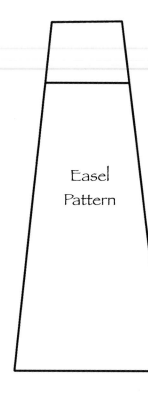

Easel Pattern

## ABCs

Add a school photo to this frame and the theme is unmistakable. Copy our design, or use the alphabet pasta to personalize with the name of your favorite student. The soft batting under the fabric adds a cozy touch.

# Time at Home

## You will need:
Round Clock
Mini houses and trees (these were from a
   children's Hanukkah set )
Artificial vine
Glue gun and glue sticks
Cardboard
Craft knife

1. Cut a piece of cardboard about 1/2" larger
than the clock face.

2. Cut a hole in the cardboard to allow for the
clockworks at back of clock.

3. Glue this cardboard to the back of the clock.

4. Lay the cardboard flat and space the
houses and trees around the clock. When they
are spaced well, glue them in position on the
edge of the clock and on the cardboard rim.

5. Glue the vine around the clock between the
houses and the clock.

6. Make a loop of the vine and glue it to the
back of the clock for a hanger.

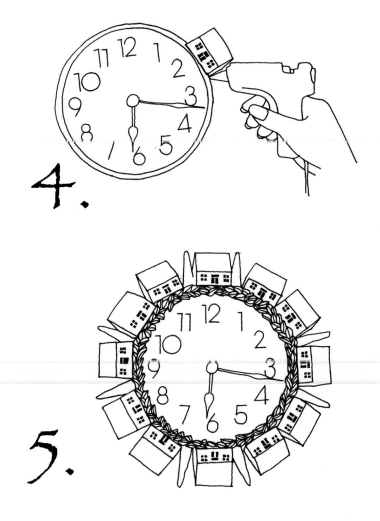

## Time at Home

A plain round clock has become a focal point on this wall with its addition of tiny houses and trees. Find miniature dwellings like this at craft shops, or use your imagination. For a child's room, you could substitute farm animals or for a kitchen, miniature pots and utensils. Even a circle of bright silk flowers would enhance this simple clock and add a distinctive note to a wall.

# All Sewed Up

**You will need:**
Cardboard frame form
Mini wooden spools
Assorted colors of floss
   or thread
Sewing themed fabric
Thin batting
Buttons - assorted colors
Glue gun and glue sticks
Craft glue

1. Cut cardboard frame form using pattern on this page.

2. Glue batting to the front of frame form.

3. Cover the frame form with fabric following the instructions for Fabric Covered Frames on page 76.

4. Wrap thread or floss around the wooden spools. Glue ends to secure.

5. Glue spools and buttons randomly on front of frame (see photo).

6. Cover back and easel with remaining fabric.

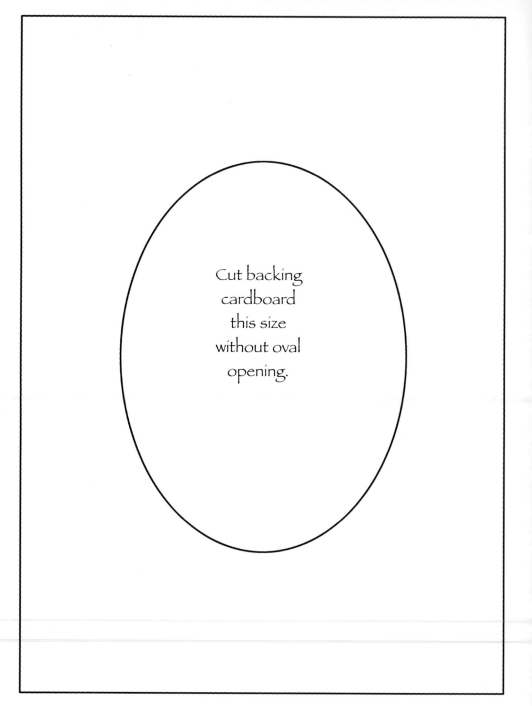

Cut backing cardboard this size without oval opening.

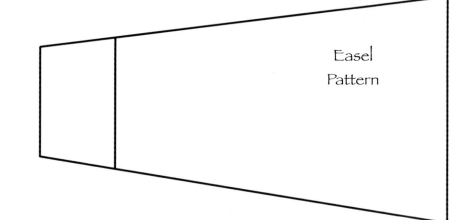

Easel Pattern

## All Sewed Up

This tribute to a favorite seamstress is decorated with familiar symbols of her pastime. Have fun with this easy project; find fabric with a sewing theme, wrap the tiny spools with colorful embroidery floss, and add buttons for a finishing touch. A thimble would be nice, too.

# Patchwork Frame

**You will need:**
Cardboard frame form
Plaid patchwork fabric
2 mini stencils
Dried apple slice
Twig
Raffia
Thin batting
Glue gun
Glue sticks
Craft glue

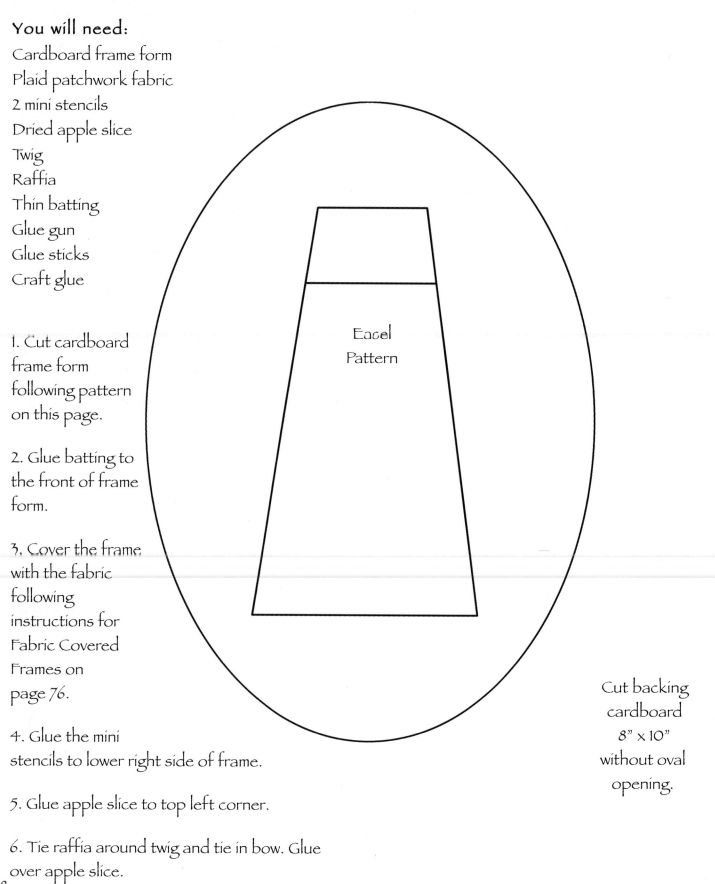

Easel
Pattern

1. Cut cardboard frame form following pattern on this page.

2. Glue batting to the front of frame form.

3. Cover the frame with the fabric following instructions for Fabric Covered Frames on page 76.

4. Glue the mini stencils to lower right side of frame.

5. Glue apple slice to top left corner.

6. Tie raffia around twig and tie in bow. Glue over apple slice.

Cut backing cardboard 8" x 10" without oval opening.

## Patchwork Frame

A patchwork of plaids covers this softly padded frame highlighting a vintage photo. Two mini stencils depict home and hearth, and celebrate the life of the couple. A dried apple slice, cinnamon stick and a bit of raffia tie up the corner, adding country flavor.

# Tortoiseshell Frame

## You will need:

Frame with wide, flat molding
Paint (Plaid) Mojave Sunset, Mustard
Decorator Glaze (Plaid) Russet Brown, Bark
  Brown, Black
Satin varnish
Splashing tool
Stippler Brush
Foam brush - 2" wide
Rubbing Alcohol
Spray bottle with water
Satin varnish
  or

Tortoiseshell Kit (Plaid) 30079
Satin varnish

1. Basepaint the surface. Let dry.

2. Brush a coat of Neutral Glaze over the surface to extend the drying time of the glaze mixtures. Mist surface with water from a spray bottle. Use the spray bottle to mist the surface as needed to keep glazes moist.

3. Dip the tips of the stippler brush in the Russet Brown glaze mixture. Pounce surface, leaving random areas without glaze. Wipe the brush bristles on a damp cloth.

4. Shake splashing tool filled with rubbing alcohol over wet glazed surface to create watermarks. Let dry.

5. Pounce surface with Bark Brown glaze mixture.

6. Shake splashing tool filled with rubbing alcohol over wet glazed surface to create watermarks. Let dry.

7. Pounce surface with black glaze mixture.

8. Shake splashing tool filled with rubbing alcohol over wet glazed surface to create watermarks. Let dry.

9. Apply varnish.

## Tip

Using a kit for faux finishing a small project is a great way to test out the technique. Other faux finish kits are available such as marbleizing, malachite, patina and verdigris. After a successful project is completed, you may want to try one of these finishes on a larger project.

## Tortoiseshell Frame

Smart, elegant and at home anywhere, this tortoiseshell project can be used to frame original art, prints, photographs or any extraordinary object. Imagine how it would look surrounding a collection of antique medals, or an old document. As an addition to a masculine room, office, or country furnished room, its effect would be stunning.

# General Instructions

## Mounting your picture

Whatever you're framing, it will need to be mounted to a board - one that won't warp and is acid-free (foam core, upson board, heavy mat board, illustration board or chip board). In most cases you will mount your art on the same size board as your picture.

**Wet Mount:** Adhesive mounting is the most common. This technique is for inexpensive prints. Apply spray adhesive evenly over the back of the artwork - then dry and press to the board. Cover the print with waxed paper and smooth it with a dry soft cloth - working from the center outwards to remove air bubbles or wrinkles. Then weigh this down and let dry overnight.

**Dry Mount**: This technique uses double backed adhesive tissue. This is an adhesive coated mounting tissue that is activated by heat and pressure. Cut a piece of tissue to the size of the art, then tack to the mounting board at two corners with a hot iron (wool setting). Position the art on the tissue with a sheet of paper over the top. Press over this on the front, then again on the back side.

If you will be framing something valuable or delicate, it should not touch the glass of the frame and should be mounted with adhesive backed linen tape at top corners.

Pastels and charcoals should also be separated from the glass with spacers around the perimeter.

When attaching art to the board with tape, it should be done only along the top edge. This prevents buckling from moisture.

## Mats

Mats are available in different thicknesses and an array of colors including metallics. Different textures are also available including linen, burlap, silk, pebbled, smooth, cork and velvet. When framing a valuable piece, acid free rag board should be used for the matting.

A very strong subject may require a large mat. It should be a related or contrasting color and texture. A delicate subject needs a subtle, plain mat.

If you are cutting your own mat, work on a clean surface and always cut from the back side.

First cut the outer dimension and then cut the opening. There should always be a wider margin at the bottom of the mat than at the top to compensate for the optical illusion of the window appearing lower than center when equal margins are used. The dimensions of the mat should never be less than 2 1/2" on the side and top and 3" on the bottom.

## Making a bevel cut

1. Lay mat face down.

2. Lay a metal straight edge on window side of the marked lines.

3. Tilt blade 60 degrees and adjust straight edge until blade hits the mark.

4. Draw the blade down the line smoothly.

5. Extend the cut 1/16" beyond the intersecting lines at each end to complete corners.

6. Push the center out.

Art supply stores sell knife guides to control the angle of the cut. Practice this technique on a scrap of mat board first.

**Hint:** If a limited edition print has a plate mark and print number it should show. So plan the mat accordingly.

## When to Use Glass

1. Don't use glass on top of oil paintings.

2. Don't use glass on needlework projects.

3. Use glass for water colors, pastels and pencil drawings and higher quality prints and photographs.

Using insulation tape on the edges of a piece helps seal the glass against the picture and will keep out dust and humidity.

If you're going to hang a picture in direct sunlight, use non-reflective glass.

## Assembling picture in the frame

Once all of the pieces are cut and mounted and the glass has been cleaned, it's time to assemble your picture. Stack as follows:

1. Frame

2. Glass, if appropriate

3. Mat

4. Picture

5. Backing board (add a stiff board for larger pieces.

   a. Run masking tape around edges to seal assembly.

   b. Lay frame face down

   c. Place assembly inside frame

   d. Carefully tack small brads to secure the piece using a flat-sided hammer.

   e. Seal the back of the assembly with heavy paper (Kraft paper works well) . Secure with tacky glue around the back edge of the frame. Lay the paper over the glue and press. Trim any excess paper with a craft knife.

## Hanging Pictures

Examine your walls to first find the correct spot for hanging and to determine if the wall is solid or hollow.

**Solid walls** - Use picture hooks which are driven into the wall with a small nail. If the wall is too hard - it will need drilling with a masonry bit. Then use a round head screw.

**Hollow walls** - If walls sound hollow - use a toggle bolt (follow manufacturer's instructions).

## Accurate positioning

1. Shaped arrangement: Hang several pictures to form a rectangle, square, or a shape the pictures fit into easily. You can leave a space in the middle of this arrangement, as long as the outer edges conform to the edges of the frames.

2. Square arrangement: When the frames are all the same size, you can easily hang them into a block. They will then be viewed as one large picture. Don't allow too much space between pictures.

3. Along a line: Hang so that all tops, bottoms or sides of pictures all line up. As in the square arrangement, don't allow too much space between pictures.

## Method 1

Hold picture level and in position on the wall and pencil in the location for the nail holes. It sometimes takes two people to do this job - one to hold the picture and the other to say "Higher on the right" or "lower on the left", etc. until the picture is even.

After the spot is chosen, lightly mark on the wall with a pencil at top of frame. Measure from top of frame to the hanger wire and mark that point below the first mark on the wall. Then hammer in the first nail. For stability hang picture with 2 nails or hooks so you don't have to straighten it often.

## Method 2

An effective way to arrange and hang your grouping is to:

1. Tape several pieces of butcher paper together the size of the area where you want to hang the pictures.

2. Lay the paper on the floor. Move the pictures around until you're happy with the arrangement. Trace around them with a pencil. Mark where the nail hole should be.

3. Tape this paper to the wall. Lightly hammer nail marks where the nails should go.

4. Remove the paper and hang the pictures.

Tip:

The mistake most often made is hanging pictures too high. Always hang pictures at EYE LEVEL or LOWER. When hanging a grouping, keep the most important pictures of the group at EYE LEVEL.

## Method 3

Use a piece of furniture or an architectural element to get a good relationship for your arrangement:

1. Between windows

2. Above sofa

3. Above mantel

4. Along a staircase

5. In a hallway

## Groups and arrangements

A large frame can hang on its own. Small frames should be hung in groupings.

Brightly painted or decorated frames should be hung on a white or neutral colored wall. A frame that is the same color as the wall may also be attractive.

Muted colors or metallic frames should be hung on a contrasting colored wall. Do not hang a multicolored frame with patterned wallpaper.

Pictures hung together as a group should be viewed as a unit. They should be related to each other in the same way. A group of family photos looks nice grouped together. They don't necessarily have to have matching frames or mats. Or a collection of impressionist prints would relate nicely together. Any collection can make an interesting grouping.

Unrelated objects can be hung together as a grouping also - but this takes a more experienced eye. The result can be a mess rather than an artistic grouping. If you're not happy with a messy grouping - try splitting up your pictures into two smaller groupings.

## Displaying Framed Pictures

Be adventuresome and hang a single picture very low and in an odd place. This will make it a focal point rather than a lonely picture hung in the center of a wall.

Try to coordinate the colors in the picture with the arrangement or area in which it will be hung.

## Ideas for Decorating Flea Market Frames

What to do with damaged frames (those you find in your attic, garage sales or flea markets):

1. Paint the frame and use a faux finish kit such as malachite or patina.

2. Age a frame even more by sanding it with coarse sandpaper or pounding it with a blunt object.

3. Decoupage with paper covering up the entire frame or parts of it.

4. Glue objects to the entire frame or parts of it such as shells, pebbles, buttons or dried flowers.

5. If you don't have paint or stain handy, a wooden frame can be stained effectively with shoe polish.

## Miscellaneous Tips

1. If you decide to use a framer, take along photos of your room so they can see your decorating style. This will help them select the proper frame and mat for your room.

2. Photographs look more artistic when framed with a very wide mat.

3. Double or triple mat a picture for greater depth.

4. To save money, use a ready made frame but have your mat professionally cut.

## Where to find prints or pictures to frame:

1. Historical societies sell photographic reproductions.

2. Buy art or photographic books at used bookstores and frame the artwork within the books.

3. Calendars (buy them on sale after the first of the year.)

4. Student art shows

5. Flea markets

6. Garage sales

7. Your attic

## Other things besides art prints or photographs to frame:

children's artwork
old maps
old magazine ads
menus
advertising cards
botanical drawings
old post cards & greeting cards
crate labels
letters
stamps
diplomas or other awards, certificates
labels
dried leaves, ferns
concert or play tickets
matchbook collections
vintage buttons

## Things to add to pictures you are framing

- doilies

- buttons

- family memorabilia

- remembrances of events

## Padded, Fabric Covered Frames

Use a heavyweight cardboard such as 300 pound illustration board.

You will be covering the front, back and easel of frame separately, then assembling.

1. Cut heavyweight cardboard using pattern for that specific project. Be sure to trace and cut both the inner and outer lines.

2. Hold the fabric tightly in place on the cardboard and turn over on table, cardboard side up. With a pencil, trace around the cardboard on the fabric, both outside the edge and inside the center opening.

3. Remove cardboard, and trim fabric about 1/2 inch beyond the pencil marks. Miter corners cutting almost to pencil-marked corners.

4. For oval or round openings, clip fabric every 1/2 inch on inside of center opening (in sunburst shape) to within 1/8" of pencil mark.

5. Place cardboard frame front on cotton batting and trace the shape, inside and out, with a felt-tip pen. Cut out and glue shape onto cardboard.

6. Place fabric on table right side down. Turn batting-covered cardboard upside down on fabric, lining it up with pencil marks on fabric.

7. Spread glue around outer edges of cardboard. Wrap fabric around outer cardboard edges and press into glue. Pull fabric as you work to keep if from wrinkling. Put a spot of glue in each corner, and work the corner fabric into it until it sticks, forming a neatly rounded corner; it will be moldable like clay. Press any loose threads into the glue.

8. Spread glue around the center opening. Pull fabric tightly into the opening, and press into glue. Pull any loose threads of fabric around to

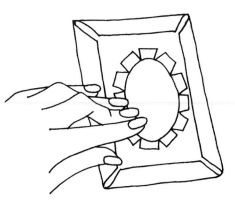

the back of the cardboard and press into glue. Push and mold the fabric into the wet glue to make smooth edges. Look at the front of the fabric to make sure cuts in the fabric are not showing; if they are, keep pulling the fabric onto the back. If you want to add lace, do it at this time; spread glue near the edge of the back of the covered frame front, and lay lace around edge, pinching extra lace at the corners. Start and end lace at center bottom, overlapping ends slightly.

9. Cover the backing cardboard with fabric. Cut the fabric as you did in steps 3 and 4, and glue as in step 7, using a thin coat of glue so it won't soak through the fabric.

10. Spread a thin layer of glue on the front side of the backing cardboard that you have just covered (this area will show through the opening in the frame). Glue on a piece of fabric that is slightly larger than the opening.

11. Cut strips of cardboard 1/2 inch wide and as long as the two sides and bottom of your frame. Glue the strips in place on the cardboard

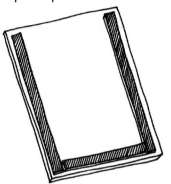

backing to form a holder for your picture (see illustration). If you wish, these strips also can be covered with fabric, at least on the outside edges and ends that will show.

12. When both front and back of frame are dry, glue them together, applying glue only to the cardboard strips around the edges.

13. Cut the easel out of cardboard (see pattern). Score (cut slightly) horizontally with craft knife about 1 inch from the top (flat end).

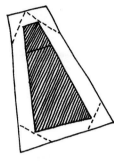

Place the easel on a scrap of fabric, and trace around it with pencil. Cut out a shape 1/2 inch larger than this tracing. Miter the corners of the fabric, (see illustration). Glue the fabric to the cardboard easel. Trace the easel shape with

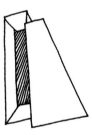

pencil onto another scrap of fabric, and cut it about 1/4 inch smaller than the pencil mark. Glue this fabric to the back of the fabric-covered easel.

14. Glue easel to back of frame

15. Add trims such as cord around edges, if desired. Use the cord to cover the spacer strips if you didn't cover them with fabric. Slide photo in position.

# Silk Ribbon Embroidery
## Transferring ribbon design to fabric

There are several ways to do this. This is the method we use. Trace the design on tracing paper. Position the design on the fabric. Tape down. On light colored fabric use a sharpened pencil and press through the paper to make pencil dots on the fabric. Make them just dark enough for you to follow the design, but not so dark that you can't easily cover it with your stitching. On dark colors use a white chalk pencil. There are also iron-on pencils that can be used.

## How to begin

Cut ribbon into 12" lengths. You may wish to press it (using low heat to remove any creases).

Needles: Use a large eye sharp needle, like a chenille needle.

## Threading and locking:

Thread ribbon through eye of needle. Pull through about 3" and then pierce the end of the ribbon (that you've just pulled through) with the needle (about 1/4" from the end).

Pull back on the opposite end of the ribbon until it locks around the eye of the needle.

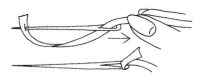

## Knotting the end of the ribbon:

Hold the end of the ribbon and form a circle with the end of the ribbon and the point of the needle. Fold the end of the ribbon down (as shown) and push the needle through the two layers of ribbon. Pull the ribbon through to form a knot.

## Wide Ribbon

Wide ribbon will sometimes fray as you pull it through the fabric. Use shorter lengths to keep it from going through the fabric very many times. If the ribbon is difficult to pull through the fabric, twist the needle as you pull it through. Don't lock the wide ribbon to the needle. This just makes it harder to pull through.

## Ending stitches:

Run needle under the backs of several stitches.

# The Stitches:

## French Knots

1. Bring the needle up at A.

2. Smoothly wrap ribbon around the needle (as many times as desired).

3. Hold ribbon securely off to one side and push needle down through fabric right next to starting point at B. Pull tightly for small French knots, very loosely for larger French knots.

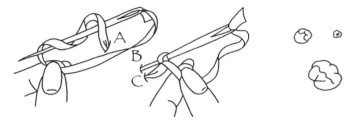

## Spider Web Rose

1. Thread needle with 2 strands of floss.

2. Work straight stitches to form five spokes. (A)

3. Thread the needle with ribbon and bring it up through the fabric at the center of the spokes. (B)

4. Weave the ribbon over one spoke and under the next. Allow the ribbon to twist and keep it loose. Keep going until the spokes are covered. (C)

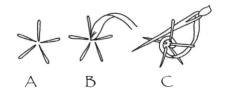

## Japanese Ribbon Stitch

1. Bring the needle up at A. Lay the ribbon flat on the fabric and push the needle back through the ribbon at B. Gently and loosely pull the needle through to the back. The ribbon will curl at the tip.

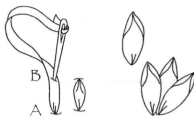

## Straight Stitch.

1. Come up from back at A. Take the desired length and go down at B. (You may make the stitch loose or taut). Make sure the ribbon lies flat. Use your thumb to hold it flat.

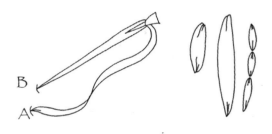

## Embroidery Stitch

### Blanket Stitch

1. Hold thread down with thumb and make a vertical stitch.

2. Bring needle over thread and pull into place. Make sure vertical stitches are straight and even.

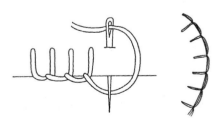

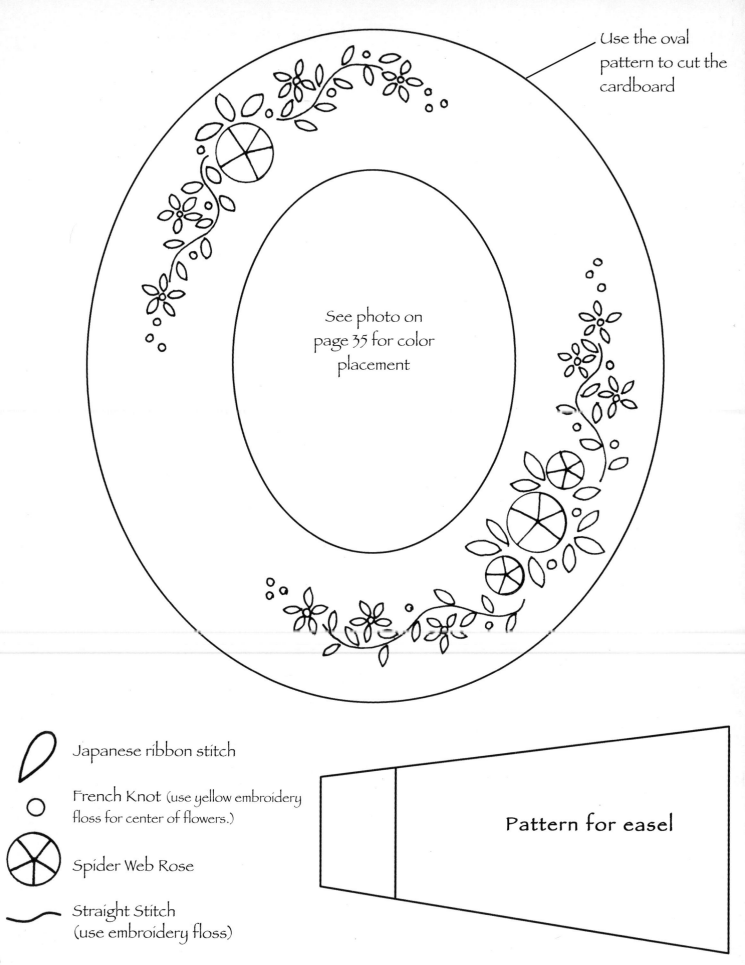

Use the oval pattern to cut the cardboard

See photo on page 35 for color placement

Japanese ribbon stitch

French Knot (use yellow embroidery floss for center of flowers.)

Spider Web Rose

Straight Stitch (use embroidery floss)

Pattern for easel